120 Poems of Love

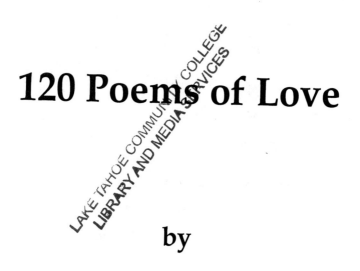
by

Richard Alan Bunch

∞ INFINITY
PUBLISHING

Copyright © 2014 by Richard Alan Bunch

ISBN 978-1-4958-0205-8

Printed in the United States of America

This is a work of fiction. Names, characters, places, and incidents either are the product of the author's imagination or are used fictitiously. Any resemblance to actual events or locales or persons, living or dead, is entirely coincidental.

Published July 2014

INFINITY PUBLISHING
1094 New DeHaven Street, Suite 100
West Conshohocken, PA 19428-2713
Toll-free (877) BUY BOOK
Local Phone (610) 941-9999
Fax (610) 941-9959
Info@buybooksontheweb.com
www.buybooksontheweb.com

To the memory of my parents

and to

Rita, Katharine, and Rick

L'amour toujours L'amour

Preface

Throughout this work, from traditional to experimental, the reader will notice continuing experiments with language, voice, imagery, form, diction, rhythm, and so forth. Welcome to these language-experiments, my poems.

Grateful acknowledgment is made to the following editors and publishers in whose publications (including online) earlier or final versions of some of these poems first appeared: *Raintown Review, Grasslands Review, Old Red Kimono, Hawai'i Review, Russian River Anthology, Voices Israel, A Hudson View, Green's Magazine, The Plaza, Studio, Red Orchids and Daffodils: Collected Poems, Latino Stuff Review, Poet's Haven, Collected Poems 1965-2011, Hidden Oak Poetry Review, Amber, The Lamp-Post, Spokes, In A Family Way Anthology, Twilight Ending, Meridian Anthology, Kennesaw Review, Poetic Eloquence, Burning Cloud Review, 42opus, Brobdingnagian Times, Suisun Valley Review, Tonight: An Anthology of World Love Poetry,* and *Snakeskin Anthology.*

In addition, grateful acknowledgment is made to my wife, Rita, for her helpful support, suggestions and also pictures of the author in each of these volumes.

Table of Contents

Times after Time

Despite the arrogant games
of fortune
where goodness counts
for nothing and
so many omens are dark,
it makes me want to paint
the soul
on the whitewall of forgetfulness.

Instead of memorizing you,
I kiss the suns
of your fingers and
the tulip of your elegant lips
and all over your body.
With such roving kisses,
you have, my sweet,
the all of me.

That is how we, times after time,
honor the power of love's fire.

Again, Love

Green is alive in springtime
Resurrections burst in daffodils.

Yes, love comes again,
The truest fire in winter

With sonnets undreamed
In lilies of genesis

That dares a kind of joy
Both essential and luminous.

Meditation at Sea Ranch

Each tangled passage, gleaned or mottled through
Contains a translucent realization:
The haunting hinges of waves crawling curved sand
Or young grass laid bare, a new sunmaiden
Bent by a tree-jesting wind, hawks with
A wing for blood aim with an aim of bread,
Cliffs sea-drenched, raptured, steeped in sun-lashed myth,
Brush yellowed, browned by rubs of late summer.

Finally, *mi alma*, the one pined for,
Bewitching, curvaceous, deeper than nights,
A kind deathless face, steamy, alluring
Lover, hankering flame, ignite into
Deafening silence this aroused screaming sea,
When my wet body slips into your sun.

Brief Light

In a rat race
of vices and follies
where talk of exotic whores
and fools is praised
and where
in a nanosecond
dust is made of maiden dreams,
our love breathes
rhyme's mazy motion
as we, with honeyed eyes,
laugh together
in this love's brief light.

Together we watch
settings of the sun's fire
and the risings of stars,
listen to wandering winds

in the tangled underwood,
drumming rain
on the roof, and
find no sound dissonant
on pearl voyages.

Such be the shining
shoulders of
our swifter-than-dreams
passion.

When Poetry is Religion

As he drinks chilly green tea
and relaxes in his gopher wood chair,
he realizes she has fed him
frail truth mixed with clever lies.

Her uncombed puffed-up-with-pride
plangent thoughts
are lost to common sense.

She does not realize
the self-sacrifice needed
to be truly a part of another's life.

For her, the moon
always shines dim.

For him, he dangles
his feet and is charmed
by coolness of the stream
even at purple dusk
when the first maple leaf falls red.

Once pinned to the sky,
he observes,
the sun dips

into the sink
and swing of the sea.

He knows the unwordable
quivers and screams
toward the silent
speech of silence.

For John Donne

Off comes
    each mistress's gown
(and lockets)
Opening your journeys
    to Jerusalem.

For God's sake
    no sadness follows
upon the heels of amour
save oughts, guilts, conceits
    of grief.

Flesh is flesh
    bone bone
the body of love
a soul's gesture
    of desire.

Dean dear, divine
    soul is the flesh's book
when love breathes
where love wakes
    and tolls the flesh.

Body's the way love
    happens long after
that other shore beckons
a first sun, remains
    of a shadow, undone.

Gorgon Lashes

It is not the flashing lashes
of the gorgons,
books thicker than elephants
in this uneven solitude,
the sound of
wistful ocarinas
or even the sea's fury
that magnifies
our frailty in the worlds
wrapped in shadows
of the ten thousand things,
but your gentle voice,
your lovely gentle voice,
breaking into dawn
that enflames and enraptures me.

In a breezy land
with purple hills
where blooming poppies thrive
and silence lies sharp
beneath a meditative sun,
fire glows
in the surrounding luster
with the glow of loving
and steady hearts.

standing with you

in the grammar of death
   where burning
mothers unending desire

where sanded cliffs
   vie to bluff
the solvent sea's resolve

where the mortar of centuries
  knees the dust
and then dissolves

as wild scrying dunes howl
  spume-spray groundless blows
past the masonry of island names

still the sea   the sea   the sea
  rises to read
the deepening moon

and with unerring
  unsteering intuition
pauses its ancient menacing

(and oddly at the address of death)

allows loves to follow love
  that utterly speaks from stones
and anchors unanchored time

Anthony and Penny

For them, love is more
than a series of
garden plot happenings
of frenzied madness.

They cherish
afternoons of feverish sweat,
the warm colors
of tender nipples,
and the naked cadences
of their embracing bodies.

Through cadenzas
of gloomy groves,

they are west and east
to each other
and savor with delight
dialects of green, sensuous
tongue kissing and enflamed
melodies of unbridled passion.

December's June

for Rita

Love is nothing
if not
thoughts of you
dripping hotter than summer.

You are love's habit
of bearing
the wintry sun
with burning ease
of stroking
my face at daybreak.

The unconquered earth
of you tempts me
to pulse on forever.

You are Mallarmé's sea breeze
gathering me
into quaffs of climbing bliss
gathering me
into sleeves of liquid desire.

Love at Fort Ross

(Czarist Russia's trading settlement on the northern
California coast [1812-41]; its last commandant,
Alexander Rotchev, was a writer, translator, poet)

we kiss on cove beach
   the coolish sun smoked yellow

hovering above turquoise
   swells, their manes curling

the fog primeval, mists billowing
   landward engulfing

kisses (you are so warm my love
   I look up:
the fort basks, its redwood
   timeless, chapel orthodox

more kisses (you are so warmly loving with
   salty breezes bathing your face
fog enshrouding vanishes the fort

   magically the fog replaying
overtures of 1840:

   Aleuts hunt sea otter
Pomo tribe members collect wild berries

   Alexander Rotchev by candlelight
pens a poem about death...

still another kiss (i dare open my eyes
   gulls squeal, sheep graze
cliffs and fort dazzle
   now reappear

yet another (i love being here with You)
   warm, watching as seals bask

8

My Omega

Our love, the liquid
moonlight's dream
between shadow and soul,
is one of the constant marvels
of eternity and
unreturning time.

Yes, we are blind as hens;
others say we drink
bottles of lies but,
remember, others are
jealous of our love.

For me, evening smiles
above cheerful hills,
and art at the pueblo.

You are my omega.
I float on a voyage
of wind above a sphere of fog.

When you are gone,
my spirit plunges downward
quiet as a black and gold leaf.

With you, I sense
your kisses rise
from the earth to enflame me.

No mere rite of spring

"Will you love me tomorrow
and tomorrow?" she asked in a blue mood.

They stood next to Brancusi's *The Kiss*
as others paused and
strolled on through the gallery.

"You, my dove, are the flower of my life,
the vision of my seeing.
You know I can't stop loving you.
Our love is no mere rite of spring.
The range and scale of my love
for you is not merely a jack of diamonds.

You have the whole deck.

With you I can fly away in darkness
and become visible
then soar home to you.
My love for you blooms and blooms
and quivers with perennials
in blinding prisms of the eternal sun."

At that point they out-kissed *The Kiss.*

Unveiling

We kiss beneath white wild stars
and open this earthly summer.

For so long I have surrendered
myself to random joys
like a sleepwalker

who fears her darker wisdoms,

her deftly-stitched bounds
between earthbound need
and castblind wish.

No longer.
Your eyes in mine
bloom into attar sloops of wind.

Memories burning with you
will upturn more bliss
than any marriage
in the mouth.

With you I will no longer reminisce
the future and its lidless griefs.

Reading Shakespeare's Dark Lady

Backtracking the centuries I
glimpse you Will cutting
through a twilit bush closing in on your dark
lady, that Moorish attraction lying between the acts
as distractions do. Your play, a foreplay
of words contours her odors,
details delicately her wired hair
for in nothing is she like the sun.
In your dun passion's suck
you don't seem to care
if her lips be coral — or where.
Your heart's iambs breathe
by the accents of embrace. You and all her
Egypt, as you take it all off this evening,
seize the summits,
as grunts shake those valleys up, your lines
making up hers, lies that in truth lie
in truth, those flatterings
your ink uses and loses
not.

11

Night Sweats

Your touch explodes
me. How can I forget bluebells
in bloom, those
cups swollen, and no less the
sweet summer grass?

A pulse this fragile, this volcanic,
takes the tyranny of dust
by the throat.

Peeling Off

The way sun spatters, spits past irony
through colored glass, or nightfall darkens a round
stone, or how thumbs when stressed blush by degrees—
these voices all hush when your love's risk has flown
downwind and left blue horses of mourning, leaves
stained sorrow, suns made of coal, bleating breasts,
worms for lips, trombones empty, all. You grieve
and rise and bleed and find in each breath death
another of your arts as death's olde thyme
steals the spice of loss, the retrieves of leaves
and engraves on your lonesome homeless charm
a new-borne will's codicil to bequeath:
you pick up your guts and from this cave go
blossom a burnt wisdom who over-knows.

Celebration for a Lover Man

In the land of naked promise
a lone drake
swims by sea-gnawed granite
and notes a shroud of mist overhangs the sea.

12

Yet he can hear bells ringing
pizzicati of the geological strings
a frenzy from the piccolos
and steady poundings of the bass drum.

It is a celebration for a lover man,
a downright turtle dove,
who dressed in red silks and
played with serpents.

Those who care for him
sprinkle stars on his coffin
and view him
next to an endless stream of flowers.

Lying Naked With Their Old Pillows

Inflaming glances of lovers
lying naked with their old pillows

in the humming looms of time
and the many, such as the

crescent moon and
water under the white heron

as she probes the avocado marsh
and the reddish furred fox

as noticed by the one,
inspire in their comings and goings

new frontiers and visionary breakthroughs
in rhymes of the sonnet and

the blue endless tapestry of their
pilgrimage through memories.

Where does it all go?

To wonder at the sun
is to fashion the world out of
a dreamer's body

blossoming that body out
into a simple flowering, including
a grape leaf, nuts, dates, and
figs and still
hear beneath roseate clouds
the moans of the
vanquished

and envisage beyond any present
sisters and brothers who
have memory's honesty
concerning life's flag that unfurls into
legends, more legends and romance
and a thousand kisses with a
thousand kisses

My Dream of You

Although you saw me
as a broken artist
with poetic flights and lips of sorrow,

and even said "adios muchacho, compañero de mi
vida,"
my dream of you with your hands
of diamonds and jewels is not over.

My love for you appears everywhere:
in dialects of flamingo under our common sun,
the bargaining of memory and forgetfulness

as sea-depths of music float over summers
past scarlet houses, hurricanes of fate,
and nights of gemini moons.

This is true as well in cities that include love's rhythms,
red crosses on white fields,
and when the sea reveals pelican mists.

Seawind in the Plums

This evening
ruffles of surf
draw out shrinking sand.
Casts of the sea pull us.

Holding you here
the rustle of your dress
seawind in the plums
the moon's cupped light.

We touch
what a wave marks-
that small world
flared up like split bone.

The sound of sound
resounding of surf
opens us
far beyond
that glib theater of the brain.
Hypnotic sea-veins
emerald fists
pull and pull
until we fast become
the underside
beauty between us.

A Bridge to Cross Over

Just as the hound of night bays
there are great circles in the sky,

marigolds on low islands,
cries of the loon,

white orchids and
ice cream dishes filled with caresses,

there is also in the
blue line cut of time

of free-born mortals a bridge
to cross over and return

having experienced the
mystical non-body

where despite trillions of sundowns
and the sea's grey desert

lauds and hosannas
show love to be all fire.

The Girl With Golden-Red Hair

In spite of the hour's flight in
this body of clay and government

officials drunk with corruption,
the sad looks of unhanged men,

and drunkards nibbling on the
illusions of each day,

drowsy with delight,
I dance with the girl with golden-red hair,

(for color always enchants) in festive
streets with an orchestra that

plays Wintertime Love, Somebody Like You,
and Endless Love,

beneath a fleet of stars
moored to seaweeds of the sky,

I find resurrection is newness
as the sun also rises again in the human heart.

Anniversaries

You cannot step twice into the same river — Heraclitus

Through this window the Russian River
reflects a shallow
smoothed out surface.
The same as last year.

And with its hush
a creamy moon
unfolds
into circles of yellow.
Much the same this time last year.

Headlights snake along the cliff-
riven coast past Jenner
then seaward to Salt Point.

We hold hands, fool around.
Seems the same as last year.

Yet we now behold newness
in sameness
when for a prolonged second
ritual's silent genius
enchants our novel eye,
speaks the speechless.

We unfold like the moon
whose shimmering
begins to echo
threads of blue syllables
intuitive cadences
of the awakening heart. Now
burns through the
undercurrents of seem. Definitely
not the same as last year.

Sunset, Kona Coast, Hawai'i

for Rita

To the south massive layers of clouds
form island mirages.
Below, lava rocks porous black
once liquid orange flame
vent Pele's volcanic dances, hissing
sulfur, ashen lunar tides,
withstand erupting turquoise surf,
dervishes of spindrift.

This setting's redorange yolk,
penciled with cloud-gray veins,
breaches that moment
when it rests lightly
on the sea
as though embracing for the first time.

We know work alone sets our suns,
snuffs out
explorations of rainbow solitudes,
eclipses the daring art.

Here we taste time
stopped, live beyond these bodies
in the way love frees, in new birds at dawn,
conversations of raindrops,
cups cracked,
plates with prints color-faded,
in the rhythmic rubbings of palm fronds.

More Frequent

More frequent are poems of tragedy
so often I write poems of joy

more frequent are poems of misery
so often I write poems of bliss

more frequent are poems of brokenness
so often I write poems of wholeness

more frequent are poems of estrangement
so often I write poems of closeness

more frequent are poems of hostility
so often I write poems of love

Surrendering His Body to Love

"Tell me with your eyes," he said,
"no more jive talkin'"
as we listened to the sympathetic strings
of that viola d'amore

and later that tenor of the poet
in *The Tales of Hoffmann*.

With jasmine on his hands, and
despite the chatter about false gods,
he surrendered his pure body to love.
Later, after we went to the greenwood
to dance and drink and sing, we eventually returned,
read the Memphis *Commercial Appeal* and
went to see the Islamic art of Samta Benyahia.
Though our days were days of pure delight,
years passed like a hankering
along a vanishing horizon line.

We were like streams on islands,
caught between a rose and the cross,
on another shore, in a native land.

Despite outward praise from friends
we could not help but notice,
our tanned and growing antiquity
between lightning strikes and a
gulf stream drying up.

Dreaming Awake

Awake dreaming is poetry
until we are ready for
the prose of sleep
when ice fills the world
and destiny rules.

I drink a cup
of the sea's blue face
in this circle of solitude
where time stills and restrains.

Your picture on the desk,
next to my pencil sharpener
and flashlight, reminds me
there are, thank goodness,
no lies between us.

I pick up my tenor sax
that leans next to the coffee table,
not for a performance,
but to remind me
that our lives
assume a sweet melody
like a marine painting
shows the restlessness of the sea.

Long After the Summer

We can melt into one another's arms
amidst days of the dead
between unconscious and conscious
silver of unknown watches
and find those summers in which we
lived as though khaki-colored hills would never
turn green with the first rains
but they will
like old letters that march
across the turns that are returns
blue moments in the flush of colors.

Advice

for Rick

1.

In your lap a love can be
and what are you doing?
Hemming and hawing
as though it could be
a thousand years!

Opportunity with a kind and true
love does not come around every day.
What will you do?

2.

Always coin of the realm
and the itch to attach and
reattach yourself
yet still not fully understand
the soul that is the real diamond.
What will you do?

Her House I Loved

I loved her house
all green and white,
with a birch tree in the front yard,
and remember how my heart
beat so fast when we kissed
on the steps and then I rode
home on my bike.

Still I remember my heart
beating so fast; it had never beat
that fast before.

I was buried in love
and forgot myself.
I had much to learn
about love as I ogled at the stars
and lost myself in Venus
in the August sky.

Piet Amadeo

was no jack-in-the box
righting wrong with wrong
popping up
among high-stepping beauties
and the loom of men
who sing of four corners of the horizon.

No, as we got to know him,
it turns out that Piet was a soul
who had grown deep
when visiting a mountain hamlet
where sparrows skylarked in the light.
That was when,
according to him,
God unmasked himself
beside a monkey-puzzle tree
pollinated by the wind.

The result was no language game
or wind-beaten verbs but
the sun's gain in a human heart,
a world within worlds where Piet
spoke of his new love in tongues
never heard before.

He had become a lover of how God
appears in human faces where all
creatures great and small
were his sisters and brothers.

The One With a Pearl Spider

From my villa, trombones slide and record
cantata chords of fire within
my long embrace with a dream lover,
the one with a pearl spider
dangling from her left earlobe
who has found her way under my skin.

She makes me know chivalry
is alive and kicking and
that I would no longer
feel dicey in the body
of a mandarin dragon.

No longer is there only a hush
in the isle of the dead
or a focus on
bone-colored moonlight's radial velocity.

During a caesura of my life
I realized a distinction
between the wordless body
of tropical fish
as distinct from a
poet's ageless love
of music's number and metaphor's words.

Standing in her sun warms my desire
for summertime in a journey of winters.

Jakinda

"Because of what we believe happened,
the past changes continuously," she said
on several occasions. She was no fossil
from paradise
where beetles dazzle in the dung.

Already she had experienced
the native nudity
of pouring water
and how land vows promises of love
to the mouth of the rivers and
why, at times, we have to
run faster than rain
until we reach a timberland of truth.

Even in the silence
of the public gardens,
she would repeat
over and over
that we
have to make space
for the light of all people.

In the tree of her lineage
her blood flowed
as virgin terrain.

She knew how much
the angel of death loves this world.

Yet just to be around her,
question marks began to chant
of God's being
as we were reminded
to fathom and cherish the holy.

Love's Body

for Rita

A bearer of peace
your mountains
ever so graced
with mists and dancing leaves;

All the playful clouds
                 of you
are peace in me,
and in your fingertips
                 God finds a way;

Ah, love, let us run
on sun bright sands

and embrace in summer spray,
shape ebony castles
and delight in suns
between our toes
and drink in
a mystic communion,
love's body.

Your arms awaiting now
the peace I am
with you.

Devotees

Spring plows turns of earth crushed slowly beneath his
moccasin feet, the moon half-showing, the scent of apple
and mint cut the salt spray, the swells of sea almost
quiet, break with a low murmur on the gravel-like sand.
Wearing blue denims, she, curvaceous, black hair hung
lightly over her shoulders like a shawl, wears spiked
heels. Refinement is an order of her blood. In the
twilight, he knows her voice, sound of the Sea of Cortez,
when she calls his name. From behind a tree, he appears
and waves: "Hola Nirvana." "My Aloha," she returns.
The sea, in its tides and time, exudes saltiness. Between
breezes, apple, mint crushed, newly-cut grasses seem a
tourniquet. In the distance, a construction crew talking,
at intervals joking like card players in a game of chance.

In turn, she, listening to the sea, the workers, calls back "My prince of Maui." The scent of apple turns more acerbic. The steady throb of the sea lulls them, the sound of chimes rides the wind, the drone of workers, all orchestral as he calls "My dove, my black Madonna." She holds grapes aloft; he comes toward her, holds her in his arms, addressing her as his dance of the cosmos. Such lovers do not die in a vineyard; they fall into a light sleep beneath odors of apple and mint newly-shorn. Dawn breaks more yellow than the persimmon tints sunset usually reports. The construction crew drones again, scything their way through layers of rock and chaos. Still he wears moccasins and one earring; she spiked heels. Between kisses in this valley of lovers, this valley of the moon, they knew night would come again. She now whispers "You are my glad tidings," He kisses her hard. The workers drone on for hours. The wheels of lingering crush more mint. Apple dreams perfume the air. Finally she says "Farewell, Time," tenderly. He adjusts a string of cowrie shells around his neck. "In some parts of this world, these count," he says with a smile. They embrace once again. The breezes seem saltier now. "Goodnight my serpent, my beautiful question." They wave again as they disappear between the mountains and the sea. For a time, that scent of apples blunts the zone of construction.

In the Valley of the Moon

I have your letter in my pocket.
As I listen to the smooth cascades
of Debussy's *Claire de Lune*,
I think how love rocks since I
memorized your face last season.
I felt as though I floated over
the bodies of summer
beneath stars of albino frost.

You were the accent of my dreams
as we viewed Hiroshige's *View of Kyoto*
and Hopper's *Nighthawks.*
You intertwine my eye and my heart
like a house of glass.

My night dreams are sunny hill days
when dreams reveal you to me.
I look forward to being with you
at the sun temples in India.
No longer am I metaphysically undone.
You know it rains in the Valley of the Moon.

Your Eyes

for Rita

Your eyes, flashes of hazel,
a tilt and dazzle of hair
and neck, a smile
as wind curved
lifts into light
among the trees and awakens in me
your touch.

Your fingers long and longer
beneath my hair, your lips
beckoning my strength
meeting yours, a phoenix vision
arising together
out of
silence.

Susanna Among the Elders

Always there is room
for beauty at three o'clock.

Even as we
chant psalms of the sun
while feeding destiny
at three o'clock.

Susanna's nakedness
curves with perfumes, braids,
and art in the blood
at three o'clock.

Her beauty unmasks
how eyes can arouse
the timeless crotch
cobra of lust.

The elders' yearning desire
shows why darkness follows
a heart of darkness.

And how innocence
blazing with light
slithers thru the tangle of lies
at three o'clock.

Love's Hottest Rock

In a world of things and
a thousand piazzas, mystical mountains,

primary colors of flying stars, ancient aliens,
the nags called love's hottest rock

and solitude's deepest circle, my only dream
all summer long was to fall asleep with you.

Yes, I did enjoy how you collect books on the web,
your trip to Grenada, your uncle's dwarf herons

and sheep that chewed snow in a forest of letters,
Kodály's *Dances of Galánta*, Mendelssohn's

Midsummer Night's Dream Suite, and
Norwegian Wood by the Beatles.

Yet my only music that crazy summer
was to fall asleep with you.

Aldo and Kalara

From the earliest hours of darkest sleep,
he dreams of painting her
beneath a Carolina moon
with strokes of a Diego Rivera
in a land where perfume fills the air
beneath soft clouds of wool.

He also dreams of playing for her
on his sax and oboe.
Arranging his notes like blossoms of fire,
they dance the bolero and tango
as two hearts meant to be one.

What unites them in their smoldering
love is not only a love-apple but doubt
diversified by faith and a marriage
feast where they do not waste time
drinking the silence of God.

Among Pages of an Old Book

an anonymous water color
of lovers who love in a way
beyond the most conventional
both with hair to the middle of their backs.

It is difficult to tell
whether it is two women or not.
The beauty of their faces, their eyes black
and amber-colored, their lips sensual,
their earrings mother-of-pearl and gold,
deviate and be lovely attractions.

Some would denounce them
yet
there are few limits to the way sensual
love may be expressed.

For My Love, Rita

Imagine us watching the sun
setting on the sea, snuggling,
even after we are gone and come
back in each other's arms.

We tips our hats to the dead,
astonish those in love, and
know our boundaries
since we do not have to suffer.

We do not change through the
seasons whether a sweltering summer
or farandole snows.

We understand how graves open
and love poet's music.

We now know every kiss and caress
survives.

31

Lucky to Love

for Rita

Lucky to have met you, my love
among the passionflowers and faces
lucky to love and love you again and
be loved here among these global caresses
of consciousness, even when we are apart.

Lucky to have met you, my love
to fondle your hands and love you
and find night sacred as mythologies of the heart
your gentle heart warm among the shooting stars
and moon guitars the dusks and dawns of our love.

Lucky to have met you, my love
to kiss your mouth with a wild heart
to ravish you tenderly as we dance
as flames aflame within sensuous songs
in starlit orchards of the night.

I Sensed Your Heart

Guiding me in dreams of summer,
not in sleep, not even forgetting,
next to mulatto fields, eggshell
mountains, and manes of the sea
and no bleeding of the sun.

I sensed your virgin hand, your
pure heart, your naked shoulders.
I count my joys when your touch
is no longer a dream
beneath a goldenrod sky.

Old Man in the Garden

Still counting the years, he ventures over
And looks for something to do.

Hoeing will do.

He stoops to light a cigarette;
Graying smoke angers his lung.

He assumes he is too old to care.

She watches him and relives her lusts, bead
After unthinking bead, fingering steps to her tattooed past.

Tulips yellow then tiptoe for red
As he hoes.

They do not even seem to notice
As I carry out the garbage.

He has something to do,
Someone to minister to.

She counts for
A few more strokes on this earth.

He is not too old
For a knowledge of flowers

And they show it
Blooming ageless in their blooms.

The Singer

Sunlight glistens in your wine
as each song mirrors the eyes of
your life that include tea-sipped mornings.

So much of your winding love and kisses
on your unblemished neck and skin of silk
swoons the listening me.

Between banana bread mornings and rhapsodies
that flower to express your soul, each song
beckons with a naked romance of you.

O sing of walks along the beach,
feel the wind, sparkle, and blue of
beach foam, for your voice,
like the dawn, rubs its ivory wings
on yellow mornings as you sing of
mountain leaves and Paris autumns.

Your kisses, hotter than tongues of evening's
rapture, in your eyes a god may be,
for even when silent your body still sings.

Distant Longing for a Woman

In training for eternity
a man of sense and learning

left alone cannot avoid the
distant longing for a woman

past memories of name after name
when one heart can become plural

for he has learned to travel light
under an azure nook of sky

where beside bonfires of music
and the sea that denudes

volcanoes and vineyards
he dreams of her

and springtime mountains
in wind gusts of nothing after nothing

along august hills
to make immortal a naked line.

A Mayan Love Song

I say jaguars
You say pumas

You say serpents
I say rattlesnakes

You say newborn maker
I say bearer hums

I say earth's water
You say sky bursts above the sea

We both speak with
the Sovereign Plumed Serpent
and join our thoughts and hearts
as one.

Talking Turkey

As the bus heads
toward the bridge
that cruises past black mountains,
the day goes down
on your atlas of pride
remembering the well-heeled stud
with a superior wit you once were.
At that time you were
the architect of
your own creative destruction.

Bone lonely, without garlands
of romance around your neck,
your hands began to turn yellow
as though you had blood
streaking your brows.

You forgot another way
to be forever young
in the words "destroy this temple"
and, like a dog,
you retuned and found
once again that buried bone.

For Grandma

To weave time tale after tale
And knit away your days,
Thinking with an hour's needles
A divinity to posses
Is to lace the yarn to you
And sleep away the ground
Of all you weave on.

Those needles are loving
Until the yarn is gone
When this ball
Has rolled into nothing.

Then you awaken
To live love's timeless tale
Or knit asleep again.

How I Loved You

until dawn
dawned and we wavered

in the light and kissed
goodnight and waved

goodbye
farewell

and I will never

Doves

They like nesting with us
in some sheltered portion
of the houses where we have lived.

Berries they love, not to mention
fruit and seeds
on autumn's ground.

A mystery about them
leaves history behind
since holy peace and spirit
arrive with them. Harmony and

love between husband and wife
emerge too.

They mesh well with
childhood gardens beneath the night
moon's opened eye and twilit forests
of origins. Joy in peace and innocence
resound their themes.

We like doves nesting with us.

Seduction

Look at you, mon frère,
just look at the price you have paid
to hold on to your long gone love.

You are made cynical by adult things,
evolved fiercely jaded, the eldest now
among the shriveled, devoid of your
once-festive humor.

Did you think for one lusty moment
there would be no justice to pay,
no dynasties to waste?

Did you not know this old way of death
is copied and daily lived all the way to
the South China Sea?

This blindness has left you eaten
by the maggots of gullibility. No wonder
you think you are saved by those
larcenous cadences you nurse.

Match on Water

In fact we are lovers. You can tell
by that delicate fidelity
lining the eyes. How we hate
when staying moments go
but remain
captured and captivated
by last gasps
of the stealing sun
coloring through layered clouds
thin as venetian blinds.

Awe and silence
hallow this setting.
We pull warmth around us
like a circle, a sacrament
of touch, of fragile space
unbroken
by that jagged brow of breakers
come to gnaw the world.

And too our eyes are bridgeable
shores of the soul's country,
our hearts rising serenely
into the body's heat, its
passion's philosophy,
its awakened aftertaste.

And the sun? In seconds
it folds into gold and
with a final swoon, slips
slowly   slowly
into a bare squint
brightening, o brightening
at the last rites
and bursts into a match on water.

Vignettes

As a soft breath
stirs the river's birch trees,
we gaze at a wall

that lists these names of the dead:
Claussen, Bunch, Svecova,
Fatalov, Moses, Glazar, etc.

I note the concern
on your face and beardless lip.

In the distance
as the polestar turns
we hear clarinets
and oboes d'amore
which help us reach
into the blindness
that makes war
into a nuclear virtue.

As we walk farther
on this sandy soil
in a flowery April,
I recount
how tender morning
visions and dreams
let a lover into my life,
not just to review undersea roses,
but to let me know
I can sing once again
as the east wind thrums
in a charming twilight.

Cherish

On a planet entwined with suburbs,
cock's foot, voiceless things, parks and vistas,
where stunted untidy days
of whore, thief, and hired guns
tangled in sea flowers and ashes
in a split-second snapshot,
step in and out of logic
within the tricks of yellowing time.

Yet in a horizon of warm moments,
thigh-penetrating glances,
and unbalanced nakedness,
I cherish the way
love survives
grief through lasting grief
and the coral red blood
of my lover's mangos and melons.

Falling Apart

"I am about to forget you," she said.
Her lover stood there
with the grit of a goddess,
listening to the moon.

"I am not fate's widow," she replied,
stirring the garlic sauce into
a meaningless motion.
Her eyes were neither thunderstruck
nor charred alive
by the lightning of this revelation.

This had been coming for awhile
in the widest circumference of shade.

The subject had been brought up before
beneath two clock faces
in the square under a sky
dimpled with whipped cream cumuli.

She had fallen for Henka the sleepwalker
whose laughter often shook her paunch
as she shopped
for stones with peaceful backs
and wild ferns.

How love winds its way
to find love, she surmised,
is one of those zodiac mysteries
that enshroud
as the season plunged into winter.

As You Walk Along

you note the fields
sprinkled with dead heroes' bones

grain and wheat of a cigar color
scrambled ages and hollowed ravines

toward the foothills that have become
wind-colored with roots music

then something stops you:
your face flowers as you envision

a young girl sleeping, a
shadow of a love that awaits you.

"I burn for him," she confessed

"I burn for him," she confessed as she kissed
The lips of the bouquet her lover gave her.
Although she knew suffering
To be the fate of bread and flesh,
She continued to pine for him.
Her father did not approve.

A halo of golden light caressed
Her father's white locks
As he walked the length of his old age
Past the shards of ancient ruins
With their midnight howls,
Clouds and birds, steady mountains,
And flowers clothed in yellow.

He smelled the sea's restless breath as he
Waited for a full sail to catch the wind
For he was bound for a
country of unfound dreams
where willows whiten, stars sing,
aspens quiver, and butterflies laugh.

Starry Nights from Afar

You will be all right long after I am
gone since the stars shone from afar
long before we arrived here, a shadow
of us, a billion stars, will remain
as far as nonsense may
be.

Remember, as you walk through
the shamrock fields of God
and glimpse
shocking coral of the afterlife

43

with its rainbow songs and laughter,
that darkness, all the way
to dream's distant music,
is only night
to eyes that look for it.

You the Man

She is the master of love's cheekbones,
    You're the master of green's astonished eye —
        He complimented the woman.

[Her avatar is the amorous song of a raven,
    Yours, a dagger of roses —
        That's what he didn't say.]

She has the cutting scent of silence,
    You, the flight patterns of desire —
        He reminded her.

[She's got a pot belly,
    You, a backbone —
        That's what he wouldn't say]

She sees through the bull's eye,
    You, through a horsepower's shadow —
        He praised her.

[She has not existed for a long time,
    You're but a murmur through laments,
        That is what he did not say.]

She meets the reality of eve in the glen,
    You, a lifetime companion,
        He repeated several times.

44

[She bleeds through the lambskin's eye,
　　You, the sorrow surgeon of daybreak —
　　　　He would not mention this.]

She is music in the sun's fiesta,
　　You, the strength of a rainbow —
　　　　He charmed her.

[It was the best he could do long after his death,
　　And it was least —
　　　　To the bitter end, true].

What's Cooking?

Gentlemen: sauté the ground
drain any excess
(kisses in your eyes)
break out the chips
(o poet of stealthy aroma)
add the sauce
(love's desire)
cook at thirty-five degrees
(lusty rhythms with romantic music bella mia te amo)
check to see if the meat is still raw
(pour the wine slowly)
Gentlewomen: when and where also
shapes the eating.

No Matter

No matter
the wrinkles,
love opens
any time!

Exile

I have been exiled into myself just as
Napoleon was exiled to St. Helena.

Day is lost in my memory.
In the mirror my face shows
zebras and ptarmigan on the move.

The cosmos is reflected in the river
and in me.

Under the sun
Seven women appear to be dancing
As though they are kachina dolls.

Five of them adore me and they smile.
Another, happily seeing me,
sings like a Tennessee Thrush.

But the seventh woman,
Stands in snow; her eyes flash
like snake eyes.

Never can she forgive me.
Revenge is her current lust.

Her face stares fiercely into my eyes
From the bottom of a beer glass:
A vow and a wedding ring.

Three Wishes

Facts can be boring, rather prosaic,
true as far as they go.

Sometimes they don't go far enough,
I want to sail away to where three wishes
may be granted since I wish for a life
without the usual pains and suffering.

46

To be able to walk and reach farther than
heart beats predicted and breathe clean air
and be alive. That's my first wish.

My second: to live in a world that is safe,
where there are no wars, murders, rapes,
and the usual plots, lies, and ego-shows.

My third wish is to be in a world where there is
genuine caring and connectedness
between folks, nature, and the animal world.

And I don't think it is wishful thinking
in a world of dust and ashes
to say I love you.

Fiona's Orchid Tattoo

As rain pokes at the window pane
unmoved in moving air,
I think of you and your orchid tattoo,
our hot love, that mystic knot
that unites us.

It is my drum skin of hope
as we note blossoms of water lilies
and listen
for voices
in the throats of dolphins.

We have endured so much:
dire strait efforts to abolish
leather-skinned locals
and the color sea-heart blue,
as we mastered fire
and inched by
eyeblinked inch
finally waltzed into grace
when the doors of darkness opened.

Solitary Man

In a season of wild love
next to a wind-swept sea

a solitary man who walks
with Andromeda and Capricorn

whose soul
is no stranger to earth,

turns away from the lairs of lying and
those wastelands of mistaken hunts

and continues to where orchards
of the resurrected meet, and finds

his heart now overflows
with sunrise.

The Luscious Woman

She is a stranger
who brings the resound of strings
to evening hamlets in our valley.

Always she seems encircled
by evening doves and the
blue and white flowers of late spring.

When you see her
white horses prance
and you rejoice that you live here.

Even every abyss radiates sunshine.
Frankly, she makes us glad
to be lustily alive.

Gifted by a Magic Wand

for Rita

Beneath the liquid skreak
Of an owl and a beside a hidden fern
My lips repeatedly whisper your name.

You invite me to have no fear, to lift up
My sails and sail to the farthest sea
Beneath soft wool clouds
and that star of fire, the sun.

As though gifted by a magic wand,
you bring out the poet and musician
Orpheus in me.

You know the best meanings are fleeting
and do not have to turn to stone;
the real freedom is poetry.

I lie among the zinnias and poppies
and dream of you.

Fanning You with a White Moon

Before we find out beneath
the lights of the hallway
leading to your cubicle
that dreaming really is copying
in the alma mater of our culture
with its blades of nothingness.

And before you
enter another order, ponder
the why of performance and
remember when you were peppy and foxy

and before I write the book of your remains
with the sad bones of my hands
I will thrum my guitar for you in
midnight snowfalls and cheer you up
during winter rains.

With a white moon fan
I will also fan you
in summers with their
mountains of sun and sophic stone.

Marica

When I first saw her,
she was the girl in the black sweater
asleep in a boat under clouds
the shade of an indigo snake.

She lived by the river that
dreams deep all the way
to the door of the sea.
A lovely farm girl with
flowing hair and seablue eyes,
when I was with her
my soul shone more pure than the sun.

She showed me how love voyages vertically
And that we really can see without hating.

We laughed and loved and she laughed
at her misspelled tattoo that read:
"thunder only happens when its raisin."

She advised me to find the me that is never mine.
It was easier than I thought.

Believe me, I am consoled by her memory.

Essays in Divinity

Cherish in yourself the birth of God.
— Meister Eckhart

What is divinity if it can come
Only in silent shadows and in dreams?
— Wallace Stevens

My last poem lying in the dark;
the nurse has left.
I feel my breathing heavy, my chest
covered with white hair.
Upon me has fallen the hermeneutic
wonder of dreams. In them, I dance
like Zorba the Greek and love women
only God's love can mystically fashion.

Evenings discover me gazing at lines
etched at the Moulin Rouge by my friend,
Lautrec.

In Athens I discuss particulars of
beauty with Plato who hankers for
souls anchored in stars.

On Lesbos, Sappho takes her girls gently
by the arm and teaches them poetry
deeper than a sigh.

Chaplain motored here this afternoon
espousing Christ and his mystic tide.

She also likes the Buddha's flower sermon
that cuts diamonds made of silk. I would

like to take tea with the lady. She does
not wear her badge like the Pharisees: her

Zen sees too far. Her prayers Om.
There is no room for her love of God.

Dreaming, I see life in other universes
and hear restaurants on the moon within

constellations of light years nearest, a
rainbow's genesis surpassing civilization.
Light stabs as curtains part. The
Physician opens my eyes galloping dream,
another pulse!

Dreams have become more real in this

last testament. What we call reality
can be a supremely fictive will, Madame.
A door softly opens:

I hear Neruda in the next age
savoring a breast of his final rose
eternally in flight.

And Tu Fu's brush concentrates:
sunsets magenta as plums inspire

each stroke higher than a man: ageless
ways words mother the fathered heart.

Nearness of end: even here dreams
clarify this orange evening

when the sun also rises
in the shape of Mexico.

The Heart of This Story

She could not get him
out of her mind
even when the soap
fell behind the bath.

And he, a son of stars,
could not forget her
seductive, tempting glances
as she put on her lipstick.

He forgot himself in the clouds
as he gazed at her.

Implicitly there was the
promise of a wedding.

Their friend, a perfect saint,
the silent one with the eternal heart,
would marry them.

At the reception
he would dance
mad as a dancer at a dancing party
in love from dawns to sea blue dawns,
and her love for him
a golden basket of diamonds.

They would honeymoon
among silver lakes and fountains
as well at the seashore.

As My Lover and I Kiss

As my lover and I kiss
next to the winding staircase,
we are hot as Greek fire
as her zoomorphic pendant
falls to the floor.

I feel the earth's rotation,
catch a scent of orange,
and unfold like a bell of colors
where wheat's golden storm
shines gold in a drench of light.

We know time squanders life
and feel the cool mossy night
and that sea's ending parish.

*

As we cool down, the distances
we stare into
are only ourselves.
We get up and shower.
And like some forgetful muse,
you still toss your charm around.

Yet the day is a mere shadow
of that passion,
a shadow who shadows
those kisses
as I begin
to assume a weighty wisdom,
and try to focus, desperately so,
on Puma Punku
and the Rama Empire of Southern Asia.

Is Fate Hooded Fire?

"Memories of you haunt me," she whispered.
She was Shoshone, who despite years of bitter
absence from her love, a Clear Lake Pomo
named Kajika, understood
truth, when egged on in a frying pan,
can be the longest soliloquy.

She often thought of him while riding
her horse Paloma. When she reined him in,
she still thought of Kajika
above the lines of hills and rincones,
hugged by the power of her passion, and
in the almond green sound of the hour
surveyed recent vineyards.

To be with him was to cherish the music,
poetry, and dances of grass.
She also knew that even in the
face of rumors, in the long run
you must feel things are true
and are true for you.

Capriccio for Solo Violin

for Rita

The fact that we, behind the masks,
were not yet lovers toast the heart
and eye's delight as we venture to a new key of C.

We could shout our love from atop a ziggurat,
from fishing sampans off Singapore,
or standing amazed at the *Flying Horse of Gansu,*
it would not even
generate comment in the *Nashville Tennessean,*

The Edinburgh Evening News,
Rome's *La Repubblica,*
The Sydney Morning Herald,
or the *San Francisco Chronicle.*

When trees weep in the rain, when
Mordred destroys Camelot, or
when Gauguin's riders
on the beach are spotted,
these generate more coverage.

But what do we care?

Whether there are voices in the dusk
on steep and lovely mountain slopes,
upward paths of dreams, days all white and blue
as daffodils bloom, or moon gazing as a
pink rose closes its petals,
there is no crack between us.

The Romance of Matilda Sharifa

Like so many, she loved the bagpipes sound
of Bonnie Scotland.
Her mouth, according to her love John Burnet,
was a wine red rose. Her omega vision of
love included cool jazz, dada, and pajama games.
He remembered showing a picture of her
to his tour guide the previous spring.
"Dat fish she for you, mon," he replied
with a broad smile.
John smiled too as he thought of the time
they played in waves by the sea.
As governments lay fast asleep,
they were happy to be alive and
to chase the saga of their future stars together.
Sitting on the beach, they watched terns
and sandpipers and kissed long and longer.

Love's Currency

When it comes to love's
fathoms of fire and waking dreams,
there are worlds within
inner worlds where you can
read sunlight and islands
with women and red flowers.

Love's currency
is a divine gesture,
an orchestra with clarinets,
bullfrogs, tympanis,
screech owls,
violas,
canopies of sky-blue,
English horns,
burgundy wine
the color of salty blood,
moonlit streets
and remembered dawns.

When Time Cracks

That goddess of love Astarte
would smile by the way
eyes of my body
whisper
my erotic flame for you.

Perhaps every love
is like that
even those beyond the seas
or as miracles
in the orchard
on summer nights
beneath a quiet moon.

It is as though time cracks,
rivers dream in the valleys
with their nymph hamlets
and suns in steady hearts.

When time cracks
we glide into lupines and bluebells,
esteem the music
of violins and ramkies,
and uncover the numinous.

Or Not To Be

Imagine my headstone
in a joyful churchyard;
barely can you scrape the moss
with your fingers to see my name
and dates in this particular galaxy
and even the word "poet" beneath it.

Or my ashes in a small corner of
a garden by a pool, now in spirit,
now in free love, with ice age
companions of sunshine, rain, snow
and thaws with rice, roses, blackberries,
rainbow colors, and the speaking
silence of the divine.

Dick and Jane

She loved his wind-tanned cheeks,
the way he played the bassoon,
danced the Polonaise,
and his lectures
on psychology
and the rediscovery
of the body as symbolic

as pomegranates.
He liked her
but was not in love with her
even after she begged him
to seduce her.

He liked her too much to do that.

He understood
that this involved
tearing her from her dream life.

But he also understood
as white sea birds know
that time resounds in the deep
and the breast
of our deepest green dreams
between nipples of starlight
dressed in the fantasia of grass.

Pandora Goes Public

Normally she wears
a bouffant wig
as she appears
in the jive talk and beat of the public.

She also knows
the torment of nothingness
since she is also a
consoler to the lonely
who need tulip-like flowerings
of an enraptured heart,
who need to find
someone to love.

Outside, a breeze unfurls
and comes sleeping

through the branches.
A lucid sun feasts
on leaves of the vine
as sunlight whispers
where she combs
her hair
sitting on the edge
of the bed.

She smiles as she thinks
of the boy she loves
who lives down the lane.

With him she wears no wig.

Black Swan

As the morning glory
blooms by the cabin
and away from the hum
of traffic and untroubled
by the earth's spinning,
you are, my love,
like hoped-for rain in a dry season.

On my noblest horse,
I think of you, my black swan,
my purple plume, and drink
the waves of your body
filled with music
and the aromas of the sea.

The light of your laughter
electrifies me with those
wild syllables of kisses.
So let us love!
Your heart can show me the way!

Glaringly Obvious

You do not have to use
an Assyrian crystal lens
to see that love
caresses all hearts
with a far and fiercer fire
than sensual closeness.

Our greenest flower,
carnal delight,
is no namby-pamby routine
but is sheer din dressed in repose.

Each day I taste
the storm on your lips
just as sure as there flow
hill breezes in the grass.

Seagulls, 1944

Ranking with the oldest of trades
they were called seagulls. They served
the fleet to the end of hand-guided seas
when prows entered and sirens tugged
at Pearl and the Philippines.

Their charms encircled as snake charmers do
young seamen. Their liberty followed
liberty with another proposition, their bodies
sleek, bejewelled, hardened in sea-hatched
breezes where mates, in their ripening unwisdom,
netted in them a shoreless dark.
When they caught sail, they spread in port.

As the anchors raised, their hearts parted
even in the face of faceless memories,

61

fading, as they sometimes do,
like silent sunbursts in snow.

They returned when the ships returned
to leave unfathomed
that circle of meat lovers bound as the tide.

The Lovers

Their profiles suggest robust
latitudes in marble, lip by lip.
Nakedness unhurried,
the bronze of repose.
But you, in the old
mercuries of joy
and grief, and I

through ticking biases
carve us
into passages
a genesis, constant
the cunning,
blemished
ends of beauty.

Homing

I celebrate you
God like the innocents

the beauty
of lovers.

So many winters
have I flung my sad nets to the sea
and lost
even the scent of your name.

Moonstruck

[based on partially imagined letters between
the author's parents]

> Driscoll Hall
> School of Mines
> Socorro, New Mexico
> March 3, 1933

Dearest DeLores,

To answer your question, that's why I'm here.
It's a chance to ride out the Depression.
I've seen bread lines snaking their way
In each town and city coming out west.
Yes, I agree, engineering may not be
As tantalizing as my darker love,
Poetry, but you know how succulent it

Is, how that bewitching siren bewitches.
Poetry so disrupts, ripples silk sheets, it
Glowers dispraise at last. I suppose each
Of us early or later has to choose
Between the fondest heart stealth or the head's
Cubed room, between triangles within and
That depressing elegy of what sure
Pays. A fact that lives: quantitative
Analysis coughs up more rewards. So do
Casting and alloys. But I must admit
Sailing those waters with you summer last
Past Portsmouth my peace was unalloyed.
To you alone my poetic cast still flows.

All that is, is for now. I wish you could
See the way clouds pink here to purple peaks.

Goodnight my moonlight madonna.

> Dreaming again,
> moi

Old Hickory Lake

Shoreline cadenzas hosted
A café of whispers.

Odors of magnolia
Encircled luminous fireflies.

Lake shadows massaged
A sleeping turtle's throat.

Our marshmallows caught fire
In the blood.

Little did we fathom
In those last kisses

How August suns are
Loves gone under the hill.

Starving Godward

Shadows of nothing yet we,
though loveless, press
the irrepressible glass
and watch the sun's arms radiate
dying to rip the dark.

Time cannot resurrect this watch
but only recounts the fight. It is we
who eclipse the spark, fish past
the way.

Boredom's where we dwell
and ensnared by despair's
latest leaves of sense
we can become unraveled
in this love
quest. Amid this all

we still can recall
the way
dark shades home.

Glass fractures but can mend
when vision enfleshes
and ends end. It traces us
with a joyful wisdom:
a graced release, islands
recast, fathoms reborn.

That elusive vision, mystical, *vita
nuova,* rejoices in the catch.
How it yields in the reluctant yielding
cornets of praise, homewards of bloom.

Between

the fury and the serene and still
a marriage that's actually
marriageable
not as sedate as
the dead still living

nor a passion
devouring the last souvenirs
of what makes us
us

but a yard
in between

where we go and plant
the feel of love
the invisible's lost kingdom

and
where I leave
to meet your planes on arriving

this cherishes us high
as irreplaceable
and allows us
to bottom low
as almost forgettable
should the unrisen arise

this is where what can be

can be on even ground
against all the undated
odds

Translation
(near Santa Fe, New Mexico)

Love is yours to translate
From the tolling vernacular rung.
Lips, tooth and tongue and all
That meaning means cannot say.

Here in the range of the Sangre de Cristos
You find love in a higher tongue
And need a ladder no longer
Than the one called silence.

A Circle of One

It flows where apples ripen.
Along the way rocks
Dissolve mirrors of snow.
It becomes a true cast

Of black spaces, dominions
That wake to lost friends,
Goodness betrayed over tomatoes.

It delights in tide pools
Where starfish stick,
Holds the hearse's wake
In a forever called the sea.
It caresses close unwashed
Silences, love does,
And tracks the
Center of the sun
In the furniture of each dark music.

The Day After

for Rita

Sunshafts flicker through a caravan
of cumuli.

Steady surf whomps and hisses
against the rocks
where mute armies of seabirds rest.

Looking up, spume-blasts shoot
through the skyline —
a brief wilderness of snow.

As you sleep, I entertain this new relation,
a rebirth in mid-sentence,
two in the incomparable
company of one.

You encircle me:
family-veins rooted all the way
through the invisible.

Today near the river's mouth
where sand itches
to meet the sea
we remember only yesterday
this wedding.

I'll cherish the sun-veins and delectable
joy in your looks long after
my bones are mountains
and salt sweetens the sea.

Existenz

Not the whole day. Not even the whole slice.
But a flare, a sunrise, however
damp. One filling of the lungs, in love's
bruised wake, and you can rise
to eat the sun.

That is what is missed
when edges are pressed out past
the urinary gold frame;
a larger understanding
can prompt you
to miss the blues
in the hands of Renoir's
woman at the piano
so you do not live your heart's summer.

Brokenness is essential,
the shorn limb that maketh whole.

Apple Dreams

Apple dreams bloom, seashells that cradle
roar at the losses.

Eyes buried long ago, you've lost

at love before (as have I)
between firesides earth and seaside sky
you sigh, you sigh dare we try
again
although there's summer hays to get lost in

and hide such longings from midsummer
roses, safe, unfound.

But hiding is to die
and not string violins in bone.

Love's best again and poetic —
can *we* roll back the stone?

Apple dreams bloom, seashells that cradle
roar at the unknown.

You See My Arms Open

I say this before all that is your world:
a fortress-fiefdom in Sweden,
blue bull tracks threading autumn,

one who needs proofs to love,
the puppet plays of Chikamatsu,
stone breakers in weatherproof boots.

You see, I become nothing but
a gravitational collapse
in time's cracked rigging-shells,
an ice crystal sleeping with uncertainty
a kitchen god nestling in the void,
or a river flowing into a nethermost wind
until I am with you.

So, you eater of ashes, fling those proofs aside
and open your mind too long asleep with death;
learn to breathe the way love sets free
in undying light
and needs no proof
in a country of spectator snow.

Tea and Biscuits

As we talk I am no longer with you
Though tea and biscuits touch my lips
And talk runs through endless sand;
We are in moments one, mystical,
Apples in horizontal arrangement.

Being there, we are not,
For the listener hears nothing call
While the eye draws its inward tongue
But gets entangled with that lesser one,
Talk of "you" and "me."

Still. Still. We are called
To compass a divinity sunslant,
That distracts us from these biscuits
As they brown, having cooled
In that state, like us.

Between Snow and Memory

From the scales of illusion, this love survives.
The rains come, the grass grows.
Snows bury, memory stokes
The smoke of myth, the bird of tongues.

The rains float, green the grass.
From the scale of illusion, our love yearns
For tongues of smoke, the birds of myth.
Memories grow as snows flow.

This love learns, scales illusion.
As grass cloaks, the rain still shows.
Snows flow the way memory knows
The bird of myth, the smoke of tongues.

The grass it grows, the rain still soaks.
Our love burns this way, embraces illusion.
The tongue learns myth, the birds of smoke.
Memories roar, foams as snow flows.

This way love learns, shreds illusion.
The rain shades, grass dries.
As snows flow, memory roams
Past myths of birds, tongues of smoke.

The rains flood, the grass hosts.
Memory saves memories though
Myth's a bird, smoke has tongues.
From illusions scaled, this love survives.

Love

as it
recedes
along a

thinning line

the taste
of overripe

mirages

Days You Died for Me

I should have known the day
roses came
anonymously. I

just thought it was a friendly
gesture. Not long after
you said you would not be seeing me

anymore.
That last night you denied and denied
even seeing them but finally
admitted
sleeping with them
all along.

In that last hug
on that last night
with goodbye blanketing our bones
in spite of promises
again on our lips, I felt like a
fish bellied up
to be cleaned
when the knife slowly slits up
the stomach from a point
behind the gills.

My eyes dropped out.

Sleepless nights and tempted
a hundred times to call you,
to feel your warmth once again, I realized
you were hard as rigor mortis.
Now in dreams
I watch your ashes in slow motion
stream endlessly
from an urn
from a plane flying low
and bouquet the tides with dust
that never will return
to the you
I once loved, once knew.

Awakening

When you needed me most,
I was sleeping.
The fish had already fed.

To hear talk about love
As though it is sugar-lined.
It is always listening, waiting,
An angling so silent it surprises
By how fast it can go.

Fine Lines

There, right there, put that finger in between
Tires worn and unborn threads: such lines melt down
Through the soot of innocence. Once so free,
The sex of history has tightly wound
Us. We don't feel deeply hate's loyalty,
Its gray intent, rank portents, savage mind,

And skies of snow? Or hear love's treachery
Illuminate the way trees pine and pine
Like fumes seething within volcanic rock?
Between time's left fist and the right's coiled wire
The body's clock suspends its tock and talk
When desire scents disdain beneath desire
And ice through fire senses *there's beauty to live*!
Living where the dead don't know they're alive.

Prospecting

With the sun at our backs, we
continue our appearance
walking
in the unmined world
past a cleavage
of crushed rock

and a sense sublime
in layers of schist.

We have no wish
for distance between us.
With hearts deeply
interfused with beauty,
our desires,
for the time being,
compass from madness
to love's crudity and tenderness.

Russian River Ode

Your waters,
beauty stretched
with momentum
and etched from pain,
are a testament.
Along your oak-sashed
shores and among
daystar-brightening pines,
barbecues, campers, and wakes
of drifting canoes, there come
aging lovers
coming home to die
like whales beached,
eaten away, their
hearts exploding.
They are lovers
who by longing
lived, some
already dead
as they die,
love's rock bleeding
up their sleeves.

Loneliness in mortal circles
mushrooms
within the algebra of twilights

for they too long
to hear
your husky throat
searing with memories
whistling through willows
and boats moored
to a truceless sky.

They too
watch children
splash and kick
those huge inner tubes
and imagine themselves
tied to the balconies of heaven.

Yours is a testament
to their courage,
to hawks that circle
in this land of initiation,
an intimacy
of an enduring kind.

Love Lost Tastes

like a postmortem sample
an autopsy performed
premature for want
of a widening vision
dreams
can ever afford
that even when floating
face down
through a thousand kitchens
of pain
there is still in those craving

lungs
snow-maned fury's air,
and in the sky's pink-orange-illumined face
horizons alive
that explode through
dead water

Naked

Bin ich ein Gott? Mir wird so licht! —Göethe

That's how it feels
standing on
these emerald waters
surrounded by diamonds.
Touching my cut lips,
cut by saying your
sacred name, a medium

no one after all
is quite able
to fathom.

All I sense
is your unimaginable
high renaissance
pursuing these bones.

I dance and dance
and fall into your paradise.
And from such emptiness
I breathe the cool
moonlit silences, gaze
into a pool-blue of maybes,
and recall your delicious
awakening words:
*have you forgotten
the unkillable love
that centers
the circumference?*

Going Alone

Kisses once real fade.
Yet you live.

Your heart's scars scar no more.

Beyond heartbreak and breathless romance
You search through all of those faces
For the one face
That connects all of the generations
Through tequila nights and arms
unarmed for loving.

No relation, only hazes flushed purple.
No caring, only posturing
As rejection proof.
Going alone, even lonelier,
So many lies, impersonal eyes
Hollow, lifeless, without compass.

At least your heart's scars scar no more.

Wedding Poem

Graced with fire and passionate resolve
to live heart by heart
may your wedding joy be a part
in the reckonings of all your days.

For you, neighbors and friends, are wed
every day as a flame
that does not die in wind or rain
but enamors with the
flow of your changing faces.

Graced with fire and passionate resolve
in all your days you can discover
understanding and this uncover:
together you can allow
each to be
and with that allowing
love one another more
as a fire rises
in understanding hearts.

For married minds, truly married,
are by freedom unbound
through that divine ground
composed heart by heart.

Seeing You Again

Beneath wakening blossoms
your smile rises
behind my eyes and down
where perches the twilight heart
that at your touch releases me.

Beside evening ponds
whose lids close the skin of night
your hand floats,
beckons these angels
swells their pulse's logic
and steps into beauty.

So many partings, dust-spumed
in white heat's midsummer
relights a drowsy recollection
of our starry beginning.

Postcards

for Rita

α.

Dearest, the night blooms radiant
in this room where stars
outline constellations
where blessings
flutter everywhere. And this a crossing over
from one side of this sphere, brain,
this furniture, to another where we feast
yes feast on the miracle of just glazed sunlight,
dragons smoking through our time blip by feverish lip.

β.

Dear, the incessant whir of the fan reminds me of a
steady wind in the pines. It has a sweep that bends to
unending. How strange to still be alive and in motion
and in motion the way currents shift their force and in a
quiet thunder lead us into a wider frame of deference.
Already we can discern sunlit bays, islands to be
spotted, seasoning of the seasons, where a universe of
kindness may be tried everywhere.

γ.

Dearest, never mind why
spring perfumes the cherry trees, squirrels leaping
limb up to limb, gold outdoing golden, or
memory deepening night.
One thing touches
the fingered instant: voices above water,
my life here with you, yes
a hunger when the lover blossoms in the lover.

Meditation at Muir Beach

Dunes in miniature wrinkle
the beach's lip as steady winds
whip the sand into beige
ribbed brows.

Whitecaps flare in rhythm;
surf tumbles into galloping
piano fingers.

A lonely gull tames her shyness;
her head tilts inquisitively
as she searches the beach.

Hers is a hunger.

Mine is how to stitch scar tissue,
another crackling of the heart,
one of love's crueler days.

Out there a hospital ship
drones seaward, its funnels
eclipse into fog. It can't
do a thing about these
drops that slowly wind
their way down my body
and color the sand redwine.

But there is in these wild waves
a peace between memories.
I can forget. I have before;
once memory and regret have
buried me in two.

After awhile the bleeding stops
as do the calls, and
like the gull, I shall fly
down the beach
and roll back out to sea.

Fury

Despite the fury
of my desire for you,
I have my heart
set on living,
not just in memories
of you
playing your scarlet guitar
or even a silence
that brings on
love-honeyed stanzas
without sense.

Through hazy summer dawns,
wind, sun and sea,
waiting for the Dipper
to rise or those times
when there was a veil
across the moon
above indigenous mountains
and eucalyptus trees,
my memories, my love,
are always of you.

When My Heart Print Bleeds

In sprays of morning my heart print bleeds red
With flint-chipped flames
For your voice breathes a sultry sonnet sound,
Your touch lures me beyond imprints of clay.

Your eyes draw kisses in blue lights
Of thighs that expose this yen's arc,
Those suns that rise along your finger tips
Nestling gently on yellowy sun-strobed waters.

81

This our dance, in honey-thirsting winds,
Revives all life from graves long lonely
With a grace unplanned as though
In a defiant fist of greener leaves, bursts us free.

Slowly

for Rita

Slowly history tingles my hands like crested dunes,
slowly delightful silences hit me when I sense primitive hunger,
slowly in the corridors of recollection, labyrinths hide me,
slowly I hate my poems, toss them to the northern and
    western winds,
slowly these bones glide past a flame into midnight seashells,
slowly down the garden path, I follow the mistress of
    sleepwalkers,
slowly on this afternoon, my body is exhumed by driven nets,
slowly docile boardwalks double in peninsulas of fog,
slowly philosophy delights in nectars of the moon,
slowly I do not know the differences between night and day,
slowly a meadow inside teases me into gulfs of sunlight, while
this love for you swells and swells that madness in the music
    I wear.

I Want to Remember

for Rita

I want to remember
your skin
that breathes

your silence
embracing the sea

your smile
a memory of home

your love
a first light of rare beauty
that lifts art
beyond readings of the blood
in windworn stones.

Fallen Leaf Lake
(May 17, 2014)

for Rita

We have come a long way
to get here
at the marina
where a huge log wrapped in chains
floats a few feet off shore.
Granite slabs line the shore.
At the end of our wooden seats,
a redwood tree stump with many rings.
The hills are awake with pine, fir, birch, poplars,
and occasional dead limbs.
Pine cones are scattered
around the boatyard grounds.

We hug.

A man and a woman
with their pitbull are here too.
Over and over the lady throws pine cones
in the water
that is so pristine
her pitbull can retrieve it.

Boat ramps bob up and down
with the breezes one moment, wind gusts the next.

Water music laps lapping the shore.
I scratch your back.

You close your eyes
and relax in the serene quietude.

I kiss your cheek. This is another world.

You and I, Love

You explore
And I dream
Of soft summer sun
In haystacks along the river.

I dream and dream
By tablespoons of the romantic sun
(Intensity's best in narrow slits)
Away from the protocols of public abuse.

You run and run.
I do too.
We run in sacred circles of summer's sun.

You explore
And I dream
The many and the one
Even when the sun's sun is winter's one.

Cool Jazz

In a hot summer of bears and tigers,
I hear you breathe, my love,
for you are part of a circle
that waits for all eight petals
to blossom as though
to lower orchid eyelids upon you.

We listen to the sea's
shouts of surf as prankish cousins
play with frisky cousins
next to those earth initials,
the waves of eternity.

You are a piano
that plays your soul's cool jazz
with notes born in the blood
of slow self-praise.

Voice Made of Dawn

Your voice made of dawn
hints at that august presence
of a life lived-in-spite-of.

I have looked for you,
it seems, forever, searched for
a freedom to live with you, love,
even at this stage
augumented by family and their reunions.

You emerge from sways of dreams,
from the paradox
that reality approaches dreams,
as you intimate a voice that,
being born so many times,
lingers not just in my mind
but in a bliss as seablue as the dawn.

Faithful Love

In the wars of love,
love's sword cuts
so as not to dilute
war with peace.
This no comedy
where pigs gobble the dawn
or sing in Strauss' *Knight of the Rose*.

On evenings of airy stillness or
those when crickets chirp
chit-chit night-night
and night-night chit-chit
or sailing on a darksome sea
or those with lightning ring
bolts of submerged shamrock,
with hearts made of earth
and seraphic hands,
true love does not dissolve
in water or is mere turf
studded with clods.

No, true love thinks
green and *light*
whereas the sensual
business and the dark
rebel in vain.

About the Author

Born in Honolulu, Richard Alan Bunch grew up in the Napa Valley. His poetry works include *Santa Rosa Plums, Rivers of the Sea, Wading the Russian River, South by Southwest,* and *Collected Poems 1965-2011.* He is the author of some stories such as "Since There's No Help," "Kismet," "Lifeguard," "Whipped Cream," and "Music City Skyline." His plays such as *Smokescreens* and *The Fortune-Telling Parrot* have appeared in several venues. His poetry has appeared in *Poetry Cornwall, Potpourri, Albatross, Riverrun, Oregon Review, Cape Rock, Hawai'i Review, Many Mountains Moving, Orbis, Windsor Review, Comstock Review, Black Mountain Review, Pinion, Tucumcari Literary Review, Nebo, California Quarterly, Whitewall Review, Hazmat Review, Poetry Nottingham, Roanoke Review, Twilight Ending, Latino Stuff Review, Fugue, Coracle, Slant, Black Moon, Heeltap, Owen Wister Review, Northwest Florida Review, Poem, Poetry Southeast, The Listening Eye, The Hurricane Review, Fire, Promise, Cold Mountain Review, Poetry New Zealand,* and *The Haight Ashbury Literary Journal.*

"(Bunch's) voice is wise and captivating, for many poems show him to be an intriguing poet with a keen connection to history, to contemporary culture, having an admirable seriousness of purpose."

— Jeffrey Levine, *Tupelo Press*

CPSIA information can be obtained
at www.ICGtesting.com
Printed in the USA
FFOW02n1544200814
6966FF